USA TODAY. TEEN WISE GUIDES

TIME, MONEY, AND RELATIONSHIPS

SCHEDULING SMARTS

How to Get Organized, Prioritize, Manage Your Time, and More

SANDY DONOVAN

TWENTY-FIRST CENTURY BOOKS / MINNEAPOLIS

Twenty-First Century Books
A division of Lerner Publishing Group, Inc.
241 First Avenue North
Minneapolis, MN 55401 U.S.A.

Website address: www.lernerbooks.com

Library of Congress Cataloging-in-Publication Data

Donovan, Sandra, 1967–
    Scheduling Smarts : how to get organized, prioritize, manage your time, and more / by Sandra Donovan.
        p.   cm. — (USA TODAY teen wise guides: time, money, and relationships)
    Includes bibliographical references and index.
    ISBN 978–0–7613–7019–2 (lib. bdg. : alk. paper)
    1. Teenagers—Time management—Juvenile literature. 2. Time management—Juvenile literature. I. Title.
HQ796.D623 2012
640'.430835—dc22   2011011850

Manufactured in the United States of America
1 – PP – 12/31/11

CONTENTS

It's easy to feel frazzled when many different things compete for your attention.

CRAZY-LIFE *Syndrome*

This has happened to you, right? You're sitting at home in front of the computer, and you're trying to write your history paper. But it's impossible to focus when you know you also have a huge literature test to study for. Plus, you have a whole pile of geometry homework

Time management strategies can help you to combat stress.

to deal with. And at some point, you should prepare for next week's PSAT exam. To top it all off, your friend keeps texting you. She wants to set up plans to see a movie this weekend. And a "friend request" e-mail from your cousin just popped up. He found you on Facebook and wants to connect.

How are you supposed to focus? How will you get everything done? It all comes down to time management. Time management tools can give you tricks to handle your unwieldy list of to-dos. And we have lots of tools to suggest. So if you're suffering from "crazy-life syndrome," keep reading. *We promise to make it worth your valuable time!*

1 WHY SO CRAZY, *Anyway?*

Stress makes it more difficult to function effectively—
and mismanaging time can increase stress.

The first thing you should know about crazy-life syndrome is that *it's not just inside your head*. And you're not the only one experiencing it. Experts have long recognized the teen years as one of life's most confusing and challenging times. Most kids enter into the teen years with their parents taking care of their needs—and telling them what to do at almost every turn. But by the end of your teens, you're officially an adult. You're able to vote, make your own decisions, and be legally responsible for your own actions. Obviously, there's a lot going on in those years from the ages of thirteen to eighteen. The teenage years are when you take charge of your own life. That's always been challenging, but modern teens often face even bigger obstacles than their parents did. *Many twenty-first-century teens are overscheduled, overexposed to technology, and overstressed.* Let's take a look at some of the main causes of crazy-life syndrome.

OVER SCHEDULED

Here's what Maria's schedule for the week looks like:

- School, Monday to Friday, 7:45 A.M. to 3 P.M.
- Homework for seven different subjects
- Tennis practice, Tuesday and Thursday, 3:30 to 5 P.M.
- Tennis game, Saturday, noon to 2 P.M.
- Orchestra practice, Monday and Wednesday, 3 to 4:30 P.M.
- Job at library, Monday and Wednesday, 5 to 8 P.M., and Sunday, noon to 5 P.M.
- PSAT study group, Saturday, 10 to 11:30 A.M.
- Volunteer at animal shelter, Friday, 3:30 to 6:30 P.M.

Besides school and homework, many teens participate in extracurricular activities such as sports and music. These extras are fun, but they make it even more important to have a good time management plan.

These teens find time to get some homework done in the library. Finding a quiet space to study and work without distractions is key.

Sometimes Maria feels as if she just can't possibly get everything done that she needs to get done. And in fact, she might be partly right. Many teens have so many commitments that it can be hard to give each one the time it deserves.

How many things are you trying to keep track of on a daily basis? Do you feel as overscheduled as Maria is? Most teens do. It's no wonder that it can be anywhere from very hard to downright impossible to fit in every single commitment every week.

Technology provides entertainment and information. But it also can be a distraction.

OVEREXPOSED

In addition to super-crammed schedules, teens are dealing with a monster of a challenge called technology. Technology really can help you get more done. Computers make research a snap—just ask your parents about going to the library to use a card catalog every time they needed to research something when they were in school. Computers also save huge chunks of time when you're writing papers, doing math, or putting together presentations. Cell phones, e-mail, texting, and instant messaging (IM) all allow you to get answers to questions in a matter of seconds.

But you probably know the downside to all this technology, right? *It's an enormous distraction.* When's the last time you were actually completely unplugged—not tuned in to the Internet, television, music, phone calls, texts, IMs, or e-mails—*on purpose?* It probably doesn't happen very often, does it? Even if you absolutely need to focus to finish a paper on time, it's hard to remove yourself from the possibility of interruption. After all, if your friends want to reach you, you want to be available, right?

The fact is, whenever you're on the computer working on a paper, you're also hooked up to IM and e-mail. And of course, social networking sites are just a click away, so you might as well see what everyone else is up to while you're working. Or maybe you should sort through your music to find some inspirational studying tunes. And then how about a small break to play that new computer game you just installed? You get the picture: technology can definitely be a huge distraction. And technology is advancing at such a breakneck speed that it can be hard to figure out how to keep it useful while stopping it from taking over your life.

If it's any consolation, teens aren't alone in this challenge. Ask any of the adults in your life, and chances are—if they're telling the truth—they'll admit that they also have trouble tuning out media and technology when they should be focusing on other things. But just because technological distractions are a universal problem doesn't mean you can't tame them. This book will give you lots of tips on how to stay on top of technology before it overtakes your time completely.

OVERSTRESSED

As if being overscheduled and overexposed isn't enough, there's one more issue complicating many teens' lives. Check in with most teens about their feelings toward school, their home lives, their finances, or their future, and they're likely to say that they feel overwhelmed and stressed out. Bet you can relate!

ATTENTION SPANS
GET REWIRED

By Marco R. della Cava

Everyone knows that our digital age—from the always-on Web to our bleeping PDAs [personal digital assistants]—is here to stay. And most users would agree that these innovations are by their very nature distracting.

Oh, hang on, an e-mail just came in. Be right back.

But just how detrimental to our powers of concentration is our penchant [liking] for ping-ponging around the Web and digesting each new tweet?

Sorry, just got the latest from Kim Kardashian. OK, we're good now. Turning off my iPhone.

All jokes aside, this question [is addressed in] Nicholas Carr's new book, *The Shallows: What the Internet Is Doing to Our Brains*. "One big triumph of human culture was the learned ability to pay attention to one thing for a long time, which the arrival of the book helped promote," says Carr, calling in from a Colorado vacation. (Carr hasn't yet developed the habit of switching off his cell phone while on break.) "But the Internet is about skimming and scanning."

"As a species, we are naturally in love with distractions," he says. "This technology is taking us back to a more primitive state. This is not a good thing."

Before anyone heaves a PC out the window and retreats to a cave, let it be known that some people disagree. Their point in a nutshell (in case you've got a call coming in): From the printing press to television, all new technologies arrive with dire warnings ("That TV will rot your brain!" anyone?), and yet people sift out the good and march on. And so we shall again.

Can we do it [turn off technology distractions]? No problem, says Rosie Navarro, 43, of San Francisco, California. As an executive assistant, she feels "so much more productive as a result of always being connected, whether that's answering a quick question by e-mail or just knowing I'm caught up." To keep from feeling too tethered to technology, Navarro sets personal ground rules that include no PDAs out on tables while meeting girlfriends or her daughter for dinner.

—August 4, 2010

Does it sometimes feel like if you take a wrong turn while writing your history paper, you're not only going to get a bad grade on the paper but you're going to fail the class, fail to get into college, and fail to be successful in life? That's an awful lot of pressure to put on yourself over one assignment—but you've probably always heard that you need to get good grades to be successful, so it can be hard to avoid panicking. Maybe your parents are super successful and you feel a ton of pressure to live up to their expectations. Or maybe your family has struggled for as long as you can remember, and you feel the weight of needing to earn money so you can take care of them. Either of those feelings can be crippling for a teenager trying to discover his or her own interests, talents, and values.

If you're feeling major pressure in any aspect of your life—at home, at school, or around friends—this book can help you put that pressure in perspective. And that's something you need to do to free up your attention for meeting your immediate commitments.

More students take AP tests

The number of students taking Advanced Placement tests has more than doubled in the past 10 years:

1.2 million

504,823

Source: The College Board

By Suzy Parker, USA TODAY, 2006

The rising number of students who take Advanced Placement (AP) exams is one sign of the growing academic pressure teens face. As this USA TODAY graphic shows, the number of teens who took AP tests shot up dramatically between 1996 and 2006. And even more students take AP exams these days.

Managing your time well means you'll have more time to spend on fun activities.

WHAT'S THE SOLUTION?

So now that you're reading about all these pressures you're facing, are you feeling more stressed out than ever? You *are* facing very real pressures. A teen's life is complicated. But you do have the power to manage your life. The key is time management. This means organizing your time so that you can get done what you need to get done and have time left to do what you enjoy.

In a nutshell, a good time management plan will reduce your stress, help you meet your commitments, and allow you to still have time left for fun stuff.

2 TREAT YOUR TIME *Like Money*

The best way to begin to manage your time is to figure out everything you have to do during a day or a week. Writing these activities down is a great first step.

$\mathcal{E}$ver heard the expression "Time is money"? People use this phrase to describe how valuable time is. What they're really saying is, "Treat your time like money, because you'll never feel as if you have enough of it." In fact, this saying is true in more ways than one. Time is valuable, and you do need to budget it just like you budget money.

But in one important way, time is *more* valuable than money. You can usually find a way to earn extra money, but you can never add extra hours to your day. You have to work with the twenty-four hours you have. This means you have to adjust your activities, your attention, and even your goals to fit into that time.

GET STARTED WITH YOUR MUST-DOS

So you want to make the most of your time and stop stressing about never having enough? The place to get started is with a **time budget**. A time budget is basically just a super-detailed schedule of everything you have going on.

The first step to creating a time budget is to make a list of all the things you must do in a week. This is an inventory of the activities you *must* budget time for. Get started by thinking about your must-dos that fall into three categories: personal care and health; school, sports, and related commitments; and family responsibilities. Think about all three of these areas.

School and extracurricular must-dos keep many teens running from place to place—not to mention family and personal-care activities!

If you start planning for just one area, you might run out of time for another. Read on to see what's included in each of the three areas.

PERSONAL-CARE AND HEALTH ACTIVITIES

These activities might seem like the least important things you do all day—after all, how are you going to finish your ten-page paper if you spend all your time eating healthful meals and sleeping nine hours a night? But in reality, you need to be healthy to accomplish anything else on your must-do list, so this is a good place to start. Personal care and health activities include

- sleeping
- eating
- bathing
- brushing your teeth
- combing your hair
- dressing

Getting enough sleep is just as important as making sure you do your homework. So plan enough time to get your z's!

SCHOOL, SPORTS, AND OTHER COMMITMENTS

This area is a biggie. The activities on this list are probably the ones you most need to organize to make sure you get everything done—and that constant barrage of school to-dos is often extra tough to get a handle on. Activities in this area include

- classes
- homework
- job
- after-school activities (working on the school paper, volunteering, etc.)
- practice (music, sports, etc.)

FULL ACTIVITY, STUDY SCHEDULES HAVE MANY TEENS JUST SAYING NO TO JOBS

By Barbara Hagenbaugh

Many teens today are working harder than ever—just not for a paycheck. Teens are studying more, are taking heavier course loads and are involved in more extracurricular activities than ever before. But the percentage of teenagers working or looking for work has steadily fallen in the past two decades.

Brian Cavanagh-Strong, 18, of Ann Arbor, Michigan, has worked [for pay] a total of three weeks in his life, but he's hardly sitting around watching reruns of *Friends*. The high school senior gets all A's and takes a heavy course load, including advanced journalism, advanced Latin poetry, a one-on-one advanced calculus course, and writing. "I am [very busy] every day until very late," Cavanagh-Strong says. "I don't think employers would be very happy with my time commitment."

For Barbara Tibbetts of Wilmington, Delaware, it makes more sense for her and her husband to help her son, Will, 16, with expenses than to expect him to find a job. "We've just decided that he's going to have to devote his time to sports and to school," she says.

Pressure to achieve—[especially] at school—is one of the key theories for why fewer teens have jobs. According to the Education Department data on sophomores, 23% said they spent 10 or more hours on homework per week in 2002, up from 14% in 1990. The more hours students spent on homework, the less likely they were to have jobs, suggesting those who aren't working are using extra time to study, not goof off.

—*August 7, 2005*

USA TODAY Snapshots®

Spending money

I work/worked after school or had a weekend part-time job for my spending money:

46% 14-20 years old

77% Over 20 years old

Source: TD Ameritrade survey of 768 adults 20-59; margin of error ±3 percentage points. 365 teenagers 14-19

By Jae Yang and Julie Snider, USA TODAY, 2009

This USA TODAY Snapshot® shows the relatively small percentage of people ages fourteen to twenty who worked for pay in 2009, compared to those older than twenty.

FAMILY RESPONSIBILITIES

Family responsibilities may not take up quite as much time as school and after-school activities, but they still demand a sizable chunk of your time. Everyone's family responsibilities differ, but they might include

- daily chores
- caring for younger brothers and sisters
- family time

Once you've made a list of your must-dos, you'll have a pretty good visual of all the essential stuff you do throughout a typical week. The next step is to figure out just how much time all that stuff takes up.

How do you do that? First, list the seven days of the week at the top of a sheet of paper or in a Word or Excel document. Then, underneath each day, record about how much time you spend on each of your must-dos on that day. The times you assign to each activity don't have to be exact. But you'll still be able to see approximately how much time you spend on each activity.

Here's an example of how your must-do chart might look when you're finished.

MON	TUES	WED	THURS	FRI	SAT	SUN
bathe/dress (1 hour)	bathe/dress (1 hour)	bathe/dress (1 hour)	bathe/dress (1 hour)	bathe/dress (1 hour)	bathe/dress (1 hour)	bathe/dress (1 hour)
breakfast (10 minutes)	breakfast (10 minutes)	breakfast (10 minutes)	breakfast (10 minutes)	breakfast (10 minutes)	breakfast (10 minutes)	breakfast (10 minutes)
commute to school (15 minutes)	commute to school (15 minutes)	commute to school (15 minutes)	commute to school (15 minutes)	commute to school (15 minutes)	soccer game (1 hour, 30 minutes)	homework (3 hours)
school (7 hours, 15 minutes)	school (7 hours, 15 minutes)	school (7 hours, 15 minutes)	school (7 hours, 15 minutes)	school (7 hours, 15 minutes)	lunch (20 minutes)	lunch (20 minutes)
band practice (1 hour)	commute home (15 minutes)	band practice (1 hour)	commute home (15 minutes)	commute home (15 minutes)	babysit (2 hours)	family dinner at Grandma's (3 hours)
commute home (15 minutes)	homework (2 hours)	commute home (15 minutes)	homework (2 hours)	homework (2 hours)	dinner (40 minutes)	sleep (9 hours)
homework (2 hours)	soccer practice (1 hour, 30 minutes)	Hebrew class (1 hour)	soccer practice (1 hour, 30 minutes)	dinner (25 minutes)	sleep (9 hours)	
dinner (25 minutes)	dinner (25 minutes)	dinner (25 minutes)	dinner (25 minutes)	clean up (10 minutes)		
clean up (10 minutes)	clean up (10 minutes)	clean up (10 minutes)	clean up (10 minutes)	synagogue with family (2 hours)		
sleep (9 hours)	sleep (9 hours)	homework (2 hours)	sleep (9 hours)	sleep (9 hours)		
		sleep (9 hours)				

FREE TIME

Now that your chart is complete, you can see how much time in your week is dedicated to your must-dos. If you're lucky, your daily must-dos will add up to less than twenty-four hours. The remaining time is yours to do with as you please (well, within reason of course). It's time to schedule yourself some free time!

Did you notice that we said *schedule* some free time? That's right—even though free time is your fun time, you'll need to schedule it into your day. This practice will help you in a lot of ways. First, by actually scheduling free time, you're guaranteeing

Free time is your time to have fun and recharge. You may do this alone or with friends. If you don't make room for free time, life may get awfully stressful!

that you'll fit it in. Second, you're acknowledging that it's important. When you know that you need to take some time to just goof off and you schedule that time, you won't feel guilty about it. And finally, having free time on your schedule will remind you that life isn't all work and no play. When you begin to feel overwhelmed, you can check your schedule for your planned-for free time.

You can learn more about creating a detailed schedule in chapter 3, but for now, you can put together a list of ways that you want to spend your free time. Call it your list of want-tos so you don't get it confused with your must-dos. Think about the things you like to do. Think about things that really relax and recharge you. Listening to music? Playing video games? Watching television? Running? Talking to friends on the phone? Everyone has different ways of relaxing. Make a list of your top ten relaxing activities and keep this list of want-tos handy for when you put together your schedule in chapter 3.

WHEN IT'S TIME TO JUST SAY NO

If your must-dos add up to more than twenty-four hours on one or two days a week, then you might have to do some reshuffling so you can fit in all your responsibilities (that is, if you have free time on other days). For instance, you might have to fit in extra homework time on Wednesdays if you have two-hour practices on Tuesdays. Or you could check with your family about moving some family commitments around so you can fit in your other activities on certain days.

Talking with a parent or other adult can be helpful if you need advice about prioritizing your activities.

But if most of your daily schedules have more commitments than hours in the day, you have a problem. You are overscheduled, and you need to take action. You might want to sit down with a parent or other adult and go over your commitments to see where you could make changes. It might be that you just need to take some focus off one activity and put more on another. Or you might need to drop one, two, or even more activities altogether.

It can be easy for teens to find themselves overscheduled. Maybe you're one of those people who always wants to fit in as much as possible. Or maybe you have a lot of interests, or you think you need to excel in a lot of different areas to get into college. Whatever the reason, being overscheduled usually means you end up doing a lot of things poorly instead of doing a few things well. Check the list of warning signs below to see if you might have an overscheduling problem. And if you do, take action. Your goal should be to get yourself to a level of commitment where you have at least a couple of hours of free time—to watch TV, hang out with friends, or just veg out—most days of the week.

WARNING SIGNS THAT YOU MAY BE OVERSCHEDULED

- You have less than half an hour of free time most days of the week.
- You wish you had more time to spend on one specific activity instead of spending a little time on many activities.
- You don't get much enjoyment out of the sports teams, groups, or clubs you belong to.
- You often feel frustrated and irritable.
- You often feel sleep deprived.
- You eat all your meals in the car on the way to school or activities.

3 MAKE A PLAN—AND *Stick to It!*

Keeping track of your day-to-day schedule is important. It helps you know what you should be doing and when.

You might be feeling a little tired of lists. So far, you've made a must-do list and a want-to list, and you charted your must-dos to see about how much time they take up each day. Whew!

In this chapter, you'll take your lists and chart and turn them into a detailed, neatly organized schedule. This will be your plan of attack for getting through your day, week, and school year while making sure you don't miss anything important. Ready to get started?

Sometimes a large homework assignment may take more than your usual homework time. You'll want to plan for such things.

YOUR DAILY SCHEDULE

For most teens, your Monday to Friday daily schedules will be pretty similar. School and homework will take up most of your time. But after-school activities and family responsibilities might make every day of the week just a little bit different. On any one day, you might have an extra family event going on, an extra-large assignment at school that's going to take more than your usual homework time, or some other kink in your schedule. Keeping a daily schedule helps make sure you're prepared for those unexpected additions to your day.

A daily schedule—a list of everything you plan to do in one day—is the centerpiece of any time management plan. Probably just about everyone you know keeps a daily schedule. It might be inside their heads, on a series of lists they jot down all day, on their phones, or in planners they carry around. But somewhere, somehow, everyone has to keep track of what they need to do each day. Here we're going to start with a basic planner. But you could also use a calendar on a computer or a phone if you'd prefer. If you go the planner route, try to find one that's about 8 by 11 inches (20 by 28 centimeters). That should be big enough to keep track of everything but light enough to carry around. Planners that show a week on every two pages *(below)* work well for many teens. Such planners let you see what you have planned for a whole week at a time.

Helpful hint: If you're in school, your days are probably pretty well organized until the after-school hours. Once you get a good schedule down, with enough hours for sleep [remember: this is crucial!] and getting ready for school in the morning, you might want to use your planner or your calendar just for the hours from when school gets out until you hit the pillow at night. But for now, plan your whole day, including the time you need to be out of bed to be really prepared—not just sleepwalking—for school. When you do this for all seven days of a week at one time, you'll be able to move some activities from super-full days into available slots on less busy days.

THE IMPORTANCE OF SLEEP

Everyone needs sleep. People who don't get enough sleep may feel grouchy and inattentive. They might also find themselves struggling to perform their daily activities, whether they're bagging groceries at work, driving to the mall, or playing sports with friends.

Sleep is particularly important for teens. Why? Teens' bodies are still growing. The human body produces many important growth hormones during sleep. In addition, most teens are pretty active. All that activity leads to—you guessed it—a greater need for sleep.

Studies have shown that teens' natural sleeping and waking patterns are at odds with school start times. Most teens have to be up pretty early for school. But teens' circadian rhythms (the patterns of your body when it comes to sleep and other biological activities) tell them to go to bed late at night and sleep late in the morning.

The good news is that there are ways you can help yourself to get enough sleep—even if you have to get up far earlier than you'd like to. Here are some ideas. See which ones work best for you.

- **Set a regular bedtime.** Then stick to it (even on weekends)! Sure, you're probably not going to get in bed at 9:30 PM on a Saturday, even if you're pretty good about doing so during the week. But if you can try to be in bed by 10:30 or at least 11 on the weekends, you're going to make it much easier on your body to get up for school on Monday morning.
- **Stay away from caffeine.** You might love to sip sodas and lattes, but the caffeine they contain is a powerful stimulant. Stimulants can make you feel wired and make it tough to catch some z's. If you find it hard to give up caffeine altogether, then try to avoid consuming it after four in the afternoon. This can go a long way toward helping you get to sleep.

- **Exercise regularly.** Exercise can help you use up energy during the day. That can make it easier to drift off at night. But the funny thing about exercise is that it gives you energy even as it uses energy up. Your energy level can feel especially high right after you've exercised. So try not to exercise too close to your bedtime. That might actually keep you awake!
- **Keep the lights low at night.** Light is a natural zeitgeber. That's a fancy way of saying that light cues your body to wake up. (It comes from the German words *Zeit*, meaning "time," and *Geber*, meaning "giver.") Light includes not just the lamps and overhead lights in your room but also computer screens, the light from a cell phone, and the glow of your TV. Stay away from all these lights in the hour before you go to bed and make sure your bedroom is dark.

Begin by filling in the activities from your must-do list. Use the must-do chart to plot out the time of day you'll tackle each activity and to figure out about how much time to allow for it. Be sure to leave at least a little bit of cushion time between activities. You can use this time to relax for a few minutes, to get from one place to another, or just to finish up a task if you didn't quite have time. You can work in your cushion time in a couple of different ways. You can overestimate the time you need for an activity, or you can actually schedule a half hour of cushion time each afternoon.

Once all your must-do activities are filled in, it's time to turn to your want-to list. Think about where each of your want-tos might fit best in your schedule and start plugging them in.

How do you determine which time slots to assign to your want-tos? Well, say one of your want-to items is running. Maybe you know that when you run, you usually cover 3 miles (5 kilometers) at a time and it takes you thirty minutes.

This teen fills in her must-dos on her PDA calendar.

34

Then you'll want to schedule running for a time when you have at least thirty free minutes. Or say the most stressful activities on your must-do list happen on Mondays. Maybe you feel that listening to music is the single most stress-relieving activity of all your want-tos. Mondays might seem easier to handle if you pencil in some time to listen to music.

Make sure to include time for the things that help you relieve stress, such as exercise. That way you'll feel more prepared for all the things you have to do.

What if you don't have enough free time in the week to add in all your want-to activities? That very well might happen. If it does, you might have to choose your favorites of the ten want-tos you identified. Or you could simply save some of the want-tos you didn't have time for and plan to do them in a different week. Having new activities to look forward to can give you a boost when you're feeling the strain of a jam-packed schedule.

Once you have your must-dos and want-tos entered into your planner or calendar, take a loozk at your weekly schedule. Were you able to fit in at least three want-tos for the week? Do you have at least nine hours left for sleeping each day? Since you can't add any extra hours to any days, you'll have to rejig your schedule a little (or maybe even a lot) if you can't fit everything in.

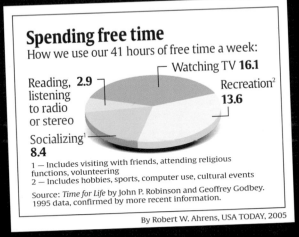

Spending free time
How we use our 41 hours of free time a week:

Watching TV **16.1**

Reading, **2.9** listening to radio or stereo

Recreation[2] **13.6**

Socializing[1] **8.4**

1 — Includes visiting with friends, attending religious functions, volunteering
2 — Includes hobbies, sports, computer use, cultural events

Source: *Time for Life* by John P. Robinson and Geoffrey Godbey. 1995 data, confirmed by more recent information.

By Robert W. Ahrens, USA TODAY, 2005

This USA TODAY graphic shows how Americans spent their free time in 2005. Many people set aside time for TV watching or recreational activities to help them unwind. These pasttimes remain popular.

A KEY TO MANAGING TIME:
PLANNING AND DISCIPLINE

By Wendy Buchert

Often, the important tasks that people need to get done get pushed aside and replaced by the easy and fun ones, according to Robert Brendel, a lecturer on time management for Towson State University in Maryland. "We disregard things that are important until they become urgent. That creates a crisis, and that's when we address ourselves to the problem," he said.

Brendel said he used to handle paperwork three or four times before doing anything with it. He couldn't meet deadlines, and he let many important things slide. "I was a classic case," he said.

Now, in addition to [teaching] and working, Brendel is studying to be a lawyer. The key to managing time: "It's a little bit of discipline, it's a lot of planning and it's forming a habit of confronting unpleasantness—those things that we like to procrastinate on."

Brendel's tips on how to have more control over your time:

- Keep a time log for one week. Every 20 minutes, jot down what you've done.
- Analyze it. Find out what your time-wasters are.
- Eliminate those things—personal and professional—that have no value to you.
- Plan for the parts of your day that you know are going to happen, perhaps four hours out of an eight-hour workday.
- Schedule things like phone calls and group similar tasks together.

When learning to manage time, "you can't do it a little at a time. You've got to keep it in the front of your mind. You've got to go out and say, 'I'm going to make a commitment to it,'" Brendel said. The result: "You get a sense of what you're doing throughout the day, rather than just doing it."

—August 3, 2010

CHANGING UP YOUR SCHEDULE

Now that you've got your schedule all planned out, you can just sit back, relax, and be organized, right? Well, sort of. Just having a schedule will save you from a lot of time wasting. You won't have to wonder what to do next, and you'll hopefully feel less panic about how you're going to fit in all the things you need to do.

But sometimes you will need to change your schedule. Maybe your family's going out of town for a three-day weekend, so you need to get some homework done early. Or maybe your marching band scheduled extra practices for a week, so you need to move some other activities around. Whatever the reason, you'll have weeks where your schedule needs to be flexible.

You'll probably have to change your schedule sometimes to allow time for special extracurriculars and other events.

Dealing with schedule changes in advance is key. You want to plan for changes instead of just reacting to them. So whenever you have an unusual event coming up, take a minute to think about how you'll need to change your schedule. For instance, are you taking Friday off school so your family can visit a relative in a different city? Then schedule some extra homework time earlier in the week. Are you going to dinner for a friend's birthday on Wednesday night? If that's going to eat into your homework time, then you'll have to move some other things around to fit it in.

Make it easy on yourself if you're using a paper planner—write in pencil when you're scheduling your week. Then you won't have to scribble all over the pages to make changes. If you're using a calendar on a computer or a phone, making changes will be a snap. Just enter them in, and you'll be good to go.

4 TAMING THE
Beast of School

Careful planning can help you maximize your study time so you can be successful in school.

*I*f you're anything like 99 percent of teens, then keeping track of and keeping up with school is probably your single biggest challenge. In fact, you may have turned directly to this chapter when you opened this book. That makes sense—school should be your biggest priority as a teen, and that means it's going to challenge you. A lot.

You probably have lots of classes with their own homework assignments, projects, tests, and quizzes to keep up with. And you probably have both short-term things to keep track of, such as that math homework that's due tomorrow, as well as long-term assignments to manage, like that science project due at the end of the year. Yikes—no wonder you're strapped for time!

But fear not. In this chapter, you can learn strategies for organizing your school life that will help keep your time management plan on track. **Remember:** the goal of a good time management plan is to be able to finish your must-dos (such as homework) so you have time for your want-tos (such as friends! and video games!).

Hopefully your school, your teachers, or your own personal experience has helped you figure out a system for keeping track of classes and homework. Maybe some of your teachers even have a required method for keeping track of assignments and other school stuff. If so, you should definitely follow their requirements or suggestions. But keep reading for additional tips and ideas—this chapter introduces one way to organize your school stuff.

If you're feeling completely overwhelmed by school—either because you don't have any organizational method or because the one you're using just doesn't seem to be working—then you can follow this chapter like a guide. *But remember there's never just one way to organize and manage your time.* You can try a bunch of different methods and see what works best for you.

THE ALL-IMPORTANT SCHOOL PLANNER

If you read chapter 3, you learned about using a planner or a calendar to schedule all your activities. Keeping track of your daily schedule—especially in those after-school hours—really is the key to managing your time well. Either an electronic device or a paper planner is great for this task.

But when it comes to tracking and managing your school-related must-dos, a paper planner is often the best choice. Why? For one thing, some students find that electronic devices don't offer a large enough viewing surface to let them see everything they need to keep track of.

For another, those devices—particularly cell phones—can be super distracting. You'll want to keep your list of school to-dos handy as you work on your homework, and having the ability to text, play games, and surf the Web right at your fingertips doesn't exactly make it easy to focus on your English assignment. In fact, some teens find that the most effective thing to do with electronic devices during homework time is to turn them off and leave them in another room. Remember: distractions are a student's enemy. After all, if you get your homework out of the way, you'll actually have time to give your full attention to texting, gaming, music, and whatever else is beckoning you.

You'll probably enjoy your electronic devices more once your homework's done and you can give them your full attention.

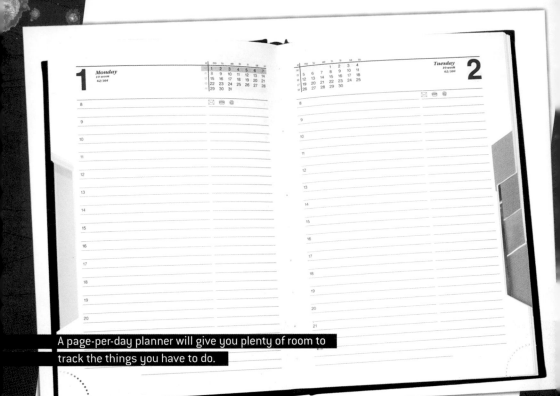

A page-per-day planner will give you plenty of room to track the things you have to do.

To be sure your school planner meets your needs, it's a good idea to choose one with a separate page for each day of the week. You're going to be keeping track of all sorts of assignments, dates, and deadlines—and one thing you don't want to worry about is trying to decipher tiny little handwriting scrawls you've tried to squeeze into too small of an area. Most office supply stores and many discount stores sell page-per-day planners. You can also find them online at specialty stores that sell calendars and planners.

Once you've found a good planner, you're halfway there. The only prep work you need to do is to spend five minutes before the start of each school week writing down your classes for each day. If you have the same classes every day for an entire semester, trimester, or quarter, this will be pretty easy. If you have a block system with different classes on different days of the week, be sure you have the right classes written down for each day of the upcoming week. You'll probably find that doing this simple task every Sunday night really helps you feel prepared on Monday morning.

When you list your subjects for each day, leave enough space to add three columns next to each subject. Label the columns "Due Today," "What I Did Today," and "To Do Tonight." Having these columns in your planner will help you track what you need to turn in when, what you covered in your classes, and what you need to accomplish in the evenings after school.

HOW MANY PLANNERS DO I NEED, ANYWAY?

So now you've got one planner or calendar to track your schedule and another to track your school assignments. For some people, this system works great. You can track the unending details of your school assignments in your school planner and keep your big-picture schedule in your other planner. But other people really like to have everything in one place. If that's you, then go ahead and ditch your scheduling planner and use your school planner to keep track of everything. Not sure which kind of person you are? Try keeping both planners for a while, and see how it works out. You can always make the switch to one planner if it seems as if that would be better for you.

DUE TODAY

The **Due Today** column can be the smallest one. This, of course, is where you write down assignments that are due on this day. This is really helpful for keeping track of due dates for long-term projects. As soon as something is assigned, flip to the due date in your planner and jot down what's due. You don't need to put any details in here. You can just say something like "final report." You can also use this column to track smaller, daily homework assignments.

WHAT I DID TODAY

This column is strictly for record keeping, but you'll find that you can save yourself a lot of time in the long run by quickly jotting down what you covered in class each day. For one thing, this can save you from endlessly flipping through your notes to find the day you covered that really confusing topic in history class. At the end of each class, write down a few key words about what you covered that day. Often you will find that you will never read those words again. But when you do want to go back and see what you covered when, *you'll be extremely glad you took the time to do this!*

TO DO TONIGHT

You guessed it—this column is for writing down the assignments or pieces of assignments that you need to finish that night. This is the centerpiece of your homework tracking. Include any details you're going to need to remember to complete your homework. For example, if you get assigned a couple of calculus problems one day and they're due the next day, write down the page number, problem numbers, or whatever else you need to know in this column.

Make sure to put your school planner in your backpack before you go to school in the morning. Don't leave it at home!

A PRIZED POSSESSION

Now, here's the most important thing about your school planner: you should treat it as if it's your most valuable possession. After all, if you want to keep up in school, get your homework done on time, and still have free time left over, your school planner *is* your most valuable possession. This means that you should always know where it is. It should be the first thing in your backpack as you head off to school every day. It should come with you to every class. It should never get left at school. And at home, it should be stored in its own personal resting spot at all times. This way you won't ever waste your valuable free time trying to track it down.

THE NO-LESS-IMPORTANT BINDER

You've probably been dealing with binders, folders, and other school supplies for years, right? Some schools or teachers even tell you exactly what type you should use. And some teens have figured out a system that works best for them. If so, then you can skip this section. But first, take this short quiz to make sure you really have it under control. If you find that any of the below statements *aren't* true for you, then read on.

- I haven't forgotten to bring home a homework assignment or other important paper this year.
- I haven't forgotten to bring a homework assignment back to school this year.
- I haven't wasted time searching for my notes to study for a test or a quiz this year.

For lots of teens, forgetting homework and losing papers feels inevitable. It happens so often that they find ways to deal

with it. But to be really successful at school, you must be organized. And unlike most of life's challenges, this one has a simple solution: binders! These tools can make all the difference in your organizational life.

There are lots of ways to organize binders, but here's one plan that works well for many teens. First, get a binder for each subject. This way, when it's time to study for history, you'll know exactly where to look for your notes. You don't need anything fancy. You can use the cheapest 1-inch (2.5 cm) binders

Keeping your school work in different binders by subject helps you stay organized.

you can find at an office supply or discount store. Next, get four tab dividers for each binder. In each binder, make four sections: notes, homework, tests and quizzes, and extra paper.

In the notes section, you'll keep all the notes you take each day. You can put your syllabus or class schedule right up front, and then start your notes in chronological order. You can either start a new sheet of paper each day or continue your notes on the same sheet from day to day. Make sure to date your notes every day. This section is also where you'll keep any class handouts. Bring them home each day and immediately punch three holes into them (if you can do this at school, even better!). Then place them in order, next to the day's notes. This system will make studying for tests and quizzes a breeze.

Then comes your homework section. You can probably guess what you put here. The key to making this section work for you is to use it. If your homework assignment is a worksheet, stick it in this section before you leave class (don't worry if it's not three-hole punched—it will stay in place until you get home). Once you complete the worksheet, get it back in its section immediately. There's nothing worse than finishing your homework and then forgetting to bring it to school on time. If your homework is another type of assignment, also make sure you place it in the homework section as soon as you're finished. Help yourself remember to do this by making sure it's in its spot before you cross it off in your planner.

You can also probably guess what to put in your tests and quizzes section. But you may be wondering why you need to save all your tests and quizzes. In fact, you don't have to save them *forever*, but you do want to save the ones from your current semester, trimester, or quarter. They can be some of your most helpful studying aids. After all, what showed up on a quiz is likely to show up on a test. And what showed up on a test is likely to crop up again on a final exam. So do yourself a favor and keep tests and quizzes organized in their section.

Finally, your last section is where you keep unused paper. This way you'll always have some when you need it to take notes in class. But take it easy on yourself! You don't need to haul around a huge supply of paper every day. Think of what that would do to your back. About twenty sheets for each class should be plenty. Check your paper supply every few days during homework time and replenish when you need to.

Speaking of taking it easy on your back, are you beginning to wonder just how heavy your backpack is going to be with all these separate binders filled with papers? Don't worry—you can keep your load low by going through your binders at the end of each semester, trimester, or quarter. Have a filing system at home for any papers you want or need to keep, and toss the rest. That way, you're carrying around only what you need each day.

GET 'READY' FOR
HONEST COLLEGE ADVICE

By Mary Beth Marklein

Robert Neuman says he has seen "every student problem imaginable" in his 25 years as an associate dean of academic advising at Marquette University in Milwaukee, Wisconsin. Now retired, he shares strategies to help middle school and high school students avoid common problems in his book *Are You Really Ready for College?* One secret, he tells USA TODAY's Mary Beth Marklein, is to start early.

Q: What's your core message?

A: College is a world very different from high school. College demands that students possess a solid, basic body of high school knowledge. They must also come equipped with the self-management skills to control the learning process. And lastly, in college, there's no time to learn how to learn.

Q: Why is "really ready" in the title? What's your point?

A: Many students enter college clueless about the level of work required of them. They believe college will be high school away from home and have a false sense of the effort needed to earn high grades in college. Studies of college-bound high school students prove the point: High school seniors study not much more than they did in middle school, yet more than half graduate with A averages. This is due, in large part, to the rampant [widespread] practice of cramming that serves so many students too well in high school but fails them in college.

Q: What's wrong with cramming?

A: Mistakenly, students think they're learning because cramming often produces good grades. Yet it yields only short-term knowledge. It lasts long enough to pass the test but fades long before teens get to college, where professors expect a solid background at the outset of their courses. Furthermore, in college, fewer tests are given, and they cover much more material, making cramming impossible. Grades plummet. Cramming is one of several student deficiencies.

Q: You make a distinction between study and homework.

A: For many high school students, simply doing homework earns them acceptable grades. Why do more? Merely doing homework does not lead to real learning. On the other hand, studying does, but it entails more: preparing for every class, besides doing homework, by rereading chapters; taking, organizing and refining notes; memorizing and reviewing; and working beyond minimum expectations. Study takes time and produces learning excellence.

Q: Could all this advice end up stressing kids out even more?

A: Much of everyday teen stress comes from being unprepared and disorganized, not having enough time, and not knowing how to handle problems. My strategies actually help relieve stress, giving teens ways to take control. Teenagers who don't learn these lessons now will become a part of the dismal statistics that universities know so well and that are becoming a topic of the national conversation. I have seen student stress firsthand in college. It's demoralizing for students and carries serious life consequences.

—August 31, 2010

HOMEWORK STRATEGY

Once you have your tools—your school planner and your subject binders—you're ready to make a homework plan. Here are some general tips for setting up a successful system for tackling your homework.

BLOCK OUT ENOUGH TIME

In your schedule from chapter 2, you should have designated some time each day to focus on homework. If you're not sure you blocked out the right amount of time, talk to your parents or teachers about how much time they think you should set aside. This doesn't mean you'll never need more time than this, and it doesn't mean you'll always use up all the time. But having a time block ensures that you'll spend at least some time every week focusing on homework. It can also keep you from always putting off your homework until later.

FIND A HOMEWORK SPOT
THAT'S RIGHT FOR YOU

This spot won't be the same for everyone. For some teens, a desk in their bedroom is ideal. Others do their best work in a home office—away from the music, magazines, and other diversions in their rooms. Still others find that spending a couple of hours every day at the local library helps them get their homework done.

USA TODAY Snapshots®

Library connections

How widely public libraries offer computer and Internet resources:

Offer access to database subscriptions (such as ancestry.com or World Book encyclopedia)	85.6%
Offer online homework resources	68.1%
Offer virtual reference	57.7%
Offer e-books	38.3%
Offer downloadable audio (such as podcasts and audiobooks)	38%

Sources: American Library Association, Libraries Connect Communities: Public Library Funding & Technology Access Study 2006-2007

By Michelle Healy and Adrienne Lewis, USA TODAY, 2008

Libraries are an ideal homework spot for many students—not only because they offer a quiet place to work but because they often have resources that most students don't have at home, such as online databases and virtual reference materials. This USA TODAY Snapshot® shows the availability of various resources in libraries in 2006 and 2007.

MAKE A HOMEWORK ROUTINE

Doing the same thing every day before you start your homework can help signal to your brain that it's homework time. It can put you in the right frame of mind to focus on your studies. You might want to unpack your backpack in the same way each day, taking out your planner first and then your books and folders, for example, and placing them on your work space in an organized fashion. Or you could get yourself a glass of water or a light, healthful snack to mark the start of a homework session.

MAKE A HOMEWORK PLAN

Take a few minutes each day to figure out what you're going to do first, second, and so on. Open your school planner, look over your tasks for the day, and figure out about how much time you're going to spend on each one. Some teens like to get their least favorite homework out of the way first. Others like to ease into homework by starting off with something simple.

BREAK IT DOWN

Have a big, overwhelming assignment looming? Rather than ignoring it, tackle it head-on by breaking it down into small tasks that you can complete in a day. Then write those tasks in your planner. By doing one small part of a large assignment each day, you get a sense of achievement as you go, and you'll avoid last-minute panic.

USE YOUR TIME WISELY

People often throw this phrase around, but it really is good advice when it comes to managing homework. Basically it boils down to making your homework time efficient. For example, if you've scheduled two hours to do homework on a Monday night but you know you can finish everything in one hour, don't just waste that extra time. Instead, get a head start on an upcoming assignment. And if you have an assignment you're not sure you understand, ask for help from an adult or an older sibling or a tutor rather than spending time worrying whether you're doing it right.

Above all, remember that there's no one way to organize your school stuff. However, almost any system is better than none! So try a few of the suggestions in this chapter and see which ones work for your particular personality.

STAY IN *Charge*

Scheduling your days and keeping on top of your priorities will help you feel in control of your time.

When you first picked up this book, you probably had a reason. Maybe you were feeling disorganized and stressed, maybe you never seemed to have the time to do what you love to do, or maybe the adults in your life were giving you grief about how you use your time. Whatever your motivation, now that you've made it to the end, you should be pretty smart when it comes to scheduling.

But you might also be feeling a little overwhelmed. You might be wondering why managing your time seems so, well . . . *time consuming!*

The fact is that a lot of small steps are involved in getting—and staying—on top or your schedule. And although these may seem as if they'll take up a lot of time, they really will save time in the long run.

Just take it step by step and keep working on getting organized. Use trial and error to discover which systems work best for you. And don't be afraid to ask for help if you need it. Teachers, guidance counselors, parents, and older siblings can all be great resources when it comes to learning how to manage your time.

When life gets really busy—overwhelmingly, ridiculously, crazy-making busy—people often feel as if they can't possibly take the time to organize their schedule. But remember that you're doing yourself a huge favor every time you take time out to get organized. If you make just one or two changes a week, you may soon find that you have more time on your hands—and suddenly getting organized doesn't feel so overwhelming.

GLOSSARY

BINDER: a three-ring notebook for keeping assignments, notes, and loose paper organized. The best school binders have hard plastic covers and fit 8-by-11-inch (20 by 28 cm) paper.

CIRCADIAN RHYTHMS: the natural patterns of your body when it comes to sleep and other biological activities

GOAL: anything that a person wants to achieve

INVENTORY: a complete list of something

MUST-DO: an activity that you are responsible for completing. For instance, most teens must keep up in school, help around their homes, and take part in family activities.

OVERSCHEDULED: to have more activities on your schedule than you have time to successfully complete

PLANNER: a notebook used for tracking appointments and other to-dos, such as tests, assignments, and projects

PRIORITY: something that is more important or more urgent than other things

PROCRASTINATE: to put off doing something that you have to do

STIMULANT: a drug that stimulates, or speeds up, the nervous system and can make it hard to get to sleep. Caffeine is a stimulant.

SYLLABUS: a summary outline of a course of study. Teachers sometimes provide their students with a syllabus at the start of a semester, a trimester, or a quarter so the students know what they'll be studying in class.

TECHNOLOGY: advanced instruments such as computers, cell phones, and PDAs that use science, math, and engineering to improve our daily functioning

WANT-TO: an activity that you want to do but are not required to complete

ZEITGEBER: a cue that tells your body to wake up or go to sleep. Light is a zeitgeber.

SELECTED BIBLIOGRAPHY

Allen, David. *Getting Things Done: The Art of Stress-Free Productivity*. New York: Penguin Group, 2001.

Dodd, Pamela, and Doug Sundheim. *The 25 Best Time Management Tools & Techniques: How to Get More Done Without Driving Yourself Crazy*. Chelsea, MI: Peak Performance Press, 2009.

Hindle, Tim. *Manage Your Time*. New York: DK Publishing, 1998.

Homayoun, Ana. *That Crumpled Paper Was Due Last Week: Helping Distracted and Disorganized Boys Succeed in School and Life*. New York: Penguin Group, 2010.

Lakein, Alan. *How to Get Control of Your Time and Your Life*. New York: Penguin Group, 1994.

MacDonald, Lucy. *Learn to Manage Your Time*. San Francisco: Chronicle Books, 2006.

Mayzler, Alexandra, and Ana McGann. *Tutor in a Book: Better Grades as Easy as 1-2-3*. Avon, MA: Adams Media, 2010.

Morgenstern, Julie. *Time Management from the Inside Out: The Foolproof System for Taking Control of Your Schedule—and Your Life*. 2nd ed. New York: Henry Holt and Company, 2004.

PBS Frontline. "Inside the Teenage Brain." PBS. 2002. http://www.pbs.org/wgbh/pages/frontline/shows/teenbrain (November 20, 2010).

Porterfield, Lisa. "Experts: Despite Their Energy, Kids Still at Risk of Burnout." CNN. 2006. http://articles.cnn.com/2006-08-30/politics/overscheduled.kids_1_homework-and-extracurricular-activities-chronic-stress-free-time?_s=PM:EDUCATION (November 20, 2010).

FURTHER INFORMATION

Adderholdt, Miriam, and Jan Goldberg. *Perfectionism: What's Bad about Being Too Good?* Minneapolis: Free Spirit Publishing, 1999. Discover if you're a perfectionist, and learn how the desire to do things perfectly can actually hinder you when it comes to managing your time.

Caldwell, Betty. *What's My Style? Test and Study Secrets for Procrastinating Teens.* Parker, CO: Outskirts Press, 2009. Do you have trouble with procrastinating? Find out more about your own learning style, and get tips for studying, test taking, and more in this book for teens.

Covey, Sean. *The 7 Habits of Highly Effective Teens.* New York: Simon & Schuster, 1998. This useful title provides readers with examples of real teens meeting their biggest goals.

Donovan, Sandy. *Budgeting Smarts: How to Set Goals, Save Money, Spend Wisely, and More.* Minneapolis: Twenty-First Century Books, 2012. Now that you've learned about organizing your time, check out this book with advice on how to organize your money to make your earnings go further.

Espeland, Pamela, and Elizabeth Verdick. *See You Later, Procrastinator! (Get It Done).* Minneapolis: Free Spirit Publishing, 2008. Check out this selection to learn how to get things done, get organized, and gain greater control over your schedule.

Homework/Study Tips: Time Management
http://homeworktips.about.com/od/timemanagement/Find_Time_to_Study.htm
This website includes tips on setting goals, organizing your homework, and more.

Hyde, Margaret O., and Elizabeth H. Forsyth, M.D. *Stress 101: An Overview for Teens.* Minneapolis: Twenty-First Century Books, 2008. Give this guide a read to get lots of effective tips on how to manage stress.

Morgenstern, Julie, and Jessi Morgenstern-Colón. *Organizing from the Inside Out for Teens: The Foolproof System for Organizing Your Room, Your Time, and Your Life*. New York: Holt Paperbacks, 2002. A well-known author of time management books for adults teamed up with her daughter to write this book especially for teens.

Moss, Samantha. *Where's My Stuff? The Ultimate Teen Organizing Guide*. San Francisco: Zest Books, 2007. This book just for teens offers great advice about a problem that's often related to managing your time: managing your stuff.

TeensHealth
http://kidshealth.org/teen
This excellent website includes a School & Jobs section that offers info on goal setting, studying for tests, dealing with homework, and other topics related to time management.

Time Management: You vs. the Clock
http://pbskids.org/itsmylife/school/time
This site covers time management topics including setting goals, choosing priorities, and making a daily schedule.

INDEX

ABOUT THE AUTHOR

Sandy Donovan has written several dozen books for kids and teens, including *Job Smarts* and *Budgeting Smarts* for the USA TODAY Teen Wise Guides series. She has a bachelor's degree in journalism and a master's in public policy and has worked as a newspaper reporter, editor, policy analyst, and website developer. Donovan lives in Minneapolis, Minnesota, with her husband, two sons, and a black lab named Fred. She wrote this book because she's never met a person who regretted having scheduling smarts—and because she hopes her two sons, Henry and Gus, will read it one day.